GARDEN NOTES

JOHN A. SALZER SEED CO'S ESTABLISHMENT, LA CROSSE, WIS.

JOHN A. SALZER
LA CROSSE, WIS.
SEED CO.

Spring 1899

SALZER'S ODDLY ODD GOURDS.

A sensational mixture of rare, strange, droll, curious, singular, comical, fantastical, queer, comely, funny, big, little, long, thin, fat, round, oblong and oddly odd shaped gourds. Just the seed you will want to plant for the children and for your own fun and pleasure. Given free with each order. See page 1.

Pkg. 20 cents; 2 pkgs. 40 cents; 1 oz. 25 cents.

Mr Cuthbert's
GUIDE TO GROWING
FLOWERING
SHRUBS

9d.

GARDEN
NOTES

...URY BELLS
...R NOW AS OUR WORLD-FAMED ANEMONES

A few of the many favourite colours in our
Latest Improved Sunshine Mixture.
(FOR PRICES PLEASE SEE OTHER SIDE OF THIS PICTURE)

REAMSBOTTOM & Co. WEST DRAYTON, MIDDLESEX.

CICO BOOKS
LONDON NEW YORK

Published in 2012 by CICO Books

An imprint of
Ryland Peters & Small Ltd
20–21 Jockey's Fields,
London WC1R 4BW
519 Broadway, 5th Floor,
New York NY 10012

www.cicobooks.com

3 5 7 9 10 8 6 4 2

Compilation © CICO Books 2012
Design © CICO Books 2012

A CIP catalog record for this book
is available from the Library of
Congress and the British Library.

ISBN: 978 1 908170 37 8

Design: Roger Hammond at bluegum
Motif illustrations: Jane Smith
Additional picture credits on
page 192

Printed in China

Contents

Chapter 1

My garden

Plot information

Use these pages to plan out your entire garden or individual beds. Make sure you take into account factors such as how much space each plant needs to grow successfully, crop rotation, and direction of sunlight. Don't forget to leave space for a compost heap and to consider where your nearest water supply will be. Your garden may also be big enough to fit in a greenhouse or tool shed so don't forget to allocate a place for them.

Location:

Dimensions:

Soil type:

Direction of sun:

Location:

Dimensions:

Soil type:

Direction of sun:

Location:

Dimensions:

Soil type:

Direction of sun:

Location:

Dimensions:

Soil type:

Direction of sun:

Location:

Dimensions:

Soil type:

Direction of sun:

Location:

Dimensions:

Soil type:

Direction of sun:

Location:

Dimensions:

Soil type:

Direction of sun:

Location:

Dimensions:

Soil type:

Direction of sun:

Location:

Dimensions:

Soil type:

Direction of sun:

Location:

Dimensions:

Soil type:

Direction of sun:

Planning your plot

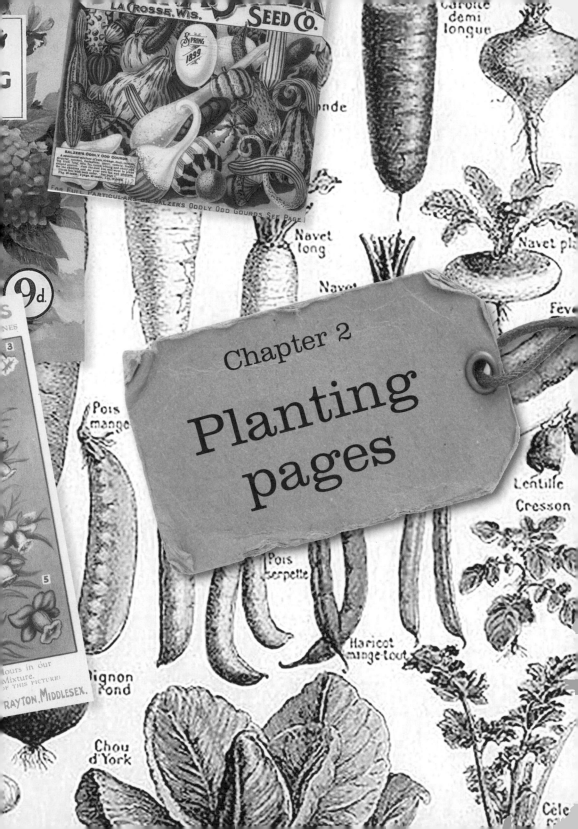

Chapter 2

Planting
pages

Flowers

Spring 1899

Every garden needs flowers in some shape or
form—whether you choose to cultivate a classic rose
garden, fill pots and containers to overflowing with
colorful bedding plants, plant up magnificent borders
with annuals and perennials, or design window boxes to
provide flowers all year round.

When buying annuals or bedding plants, it's very easy to
forget which varieties have been successful in your garden,
so use the following pages to keep a record of what you have
planted. If you like to cultivate colorful displays of springtime
bulbs, keep a note of what you have planted where—this will
prevent you accidentally digging up bulbs that have started
to grow.

From zingy nasturtiums to colorful aquilegias and delicate
honesty, many flowers produce copious amounts of seed. Once
the seedheads have developed, you can either leave them for the
wind to scatter the seed around your garden or you can pick the
seedheads, place them in a paper bag, and leave them to dry out.
Store the seeds that drop from the dried seedheads in envelopes
labeled with the plant name, and you will be ready to grow your
own flowers from seed the following year. When growing from
seed, keep a record of how long the seeds take to germinate
and resist the temptation to plant out seedlings until
any danger of overnight frost has passed. And if you
find that all your seedlings have grown on and you
have more than you need, swap plants with other keen
gardeners to extend the range of flowers in your garden.

Annuals

Flower name: _____

Variety planted: _____

Seeds sown: _____

Germination period: _____

Seedlings planted out: _____

Location: _____

Comments: _____

_____

_____

_____

Flower name: _____

Variety planted: _____

Seeds sown: _____

Germination period: _____

Seedlings planted out: _____

Location: _____

Comments: _____

_____

_____

_____

Flower name: _____

Variety planted: _____

Seeds sown: _____

Germination period: _____

Seedlings planted out: _____

Location: _____

Comments: _____

_____

_____

_____

Flower name:

Variety planted:

Seeds sown:

Germination period:

Seedlings planted out:

Location:

Comments:

Flower name:

Variety planted:

Seeds sown:

Germination period:

Seedlings planted out:

Location:

Comments:

Flower name:

Variety planted:

Seeds sown:

Germination period:

Seedlings planted out:

Location:

Comments:

Annuals

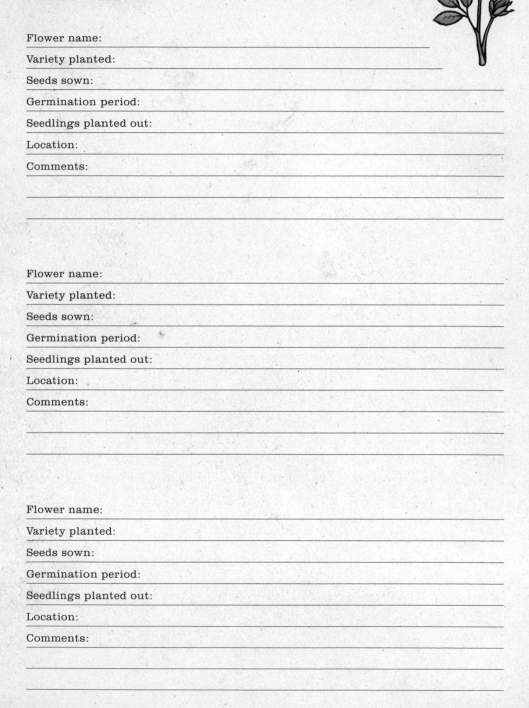

Flower name:

Variety planted:

Seeds sown:

Germination period:

Seedlings planted out:

Location:

Comments:

Flower name:

Variety planted:

Seeds sown:

Germination period:

Seedlings planted out:

Location:

Comments:

Flower name:

Variety planted:

Seeds sown:

Germination period:

Seedlings planted out:

Location:

Comments:

Flower name: _____

Variety planted: _____

Seeds sown: _____

Germination period: _____

Seedlings planted out: _____

Location: _____

Comments: _____

_____

_____

Flower name: _____

Variety planted: _____

Seeds sown: _____

Germination period: _____

Seedlings planted out: _____

Location: _____

Comments: _____

_____

_____

Flower name: _____

Variety planted: _____

Seeds sown: _____

Germination period: _____

Seedlings planted out: _____

Location: _____

Comments: _____

_____

_____

Annuals

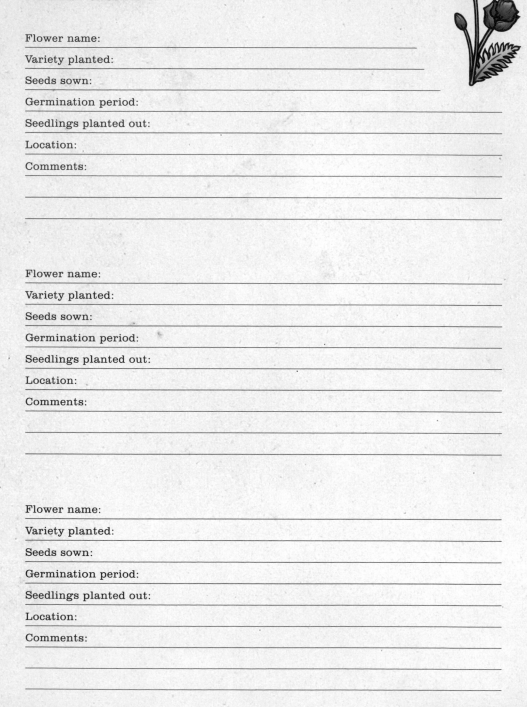

Flower name: _____

Variety planted: _____

Seeds sown: _____

Germination period: _____

Seedlings planted out: _____

Location: _____

Comments: _____

_____

_____

Flower name: _____

Variety planted: _____

Seeds sown: _____

Germination period: _____

Seedlings planted out: _____

Location: _____

Comments: _____

_____

_____

Flower name: _____

Variety planted: _____

Seeds sown: _____

Germination period: _____

Seedlings planted out: _____

Location: _____

Comments: _____

_____

_____

Flower name: _____

Variety planted: _____

Seeds sown: _____

Germination period: _____

Seedlings planted out: _____

Location: _____

Comments: _____

_____

_____

Flower name: _____

Variety planted: _____

Seeds sown: _____

Germination period: _____

Seedlings planted out: _____

Location: _____

Comments: _____

_____

_____

Flower name: _____

Variety planted: _____

Seeds sown: _____

Germination period: _____

Seedlings planted out: _____

Location: _____

Comments: _____

_____

_____

Annuals

Flower name:

Variety planted:

Seeds sown:

Germination period:

Seedlings planted out:

Location:

Comments:

Flower name:

Variety planted:

Seeds sown:

Germination period:

Seedlings planted out:

Location:

Comments:

Flower name:

Variety planted:

Seeds sown:

Germination period:

Seedlings planted out:

Location:

Comments:

Flower name: _____

Variety planted: _____

Seeds sown: _____

Germination period: _____

Seedlings planted out: _____

Location: _____

Comments: _____

_____

_____

Flower name: _____

Variety planted: _____

Seeds sown: _____

Germination period: _____

Seedlings planted out: _____

Location: _____

Comments: _____

_____

_____

Flower name: _____

Variety planted: _____

Seeds sown: _____

Germination period: _____

Seedlings planted out: _____

Location: _____

Comments: _____

_____

Perennials

Flower name:

Variety planted:

Seeds sown:

Germination period:

Seedlings planted out:

Location:

Comments:

Flower name:

Variety planted:

Seeds sown:

Germination period:

Seedlings planted out:

Location:

Comments:

Flower name:

Variety planted:

Seeds sown:

Germination period:

Seedlings planted out:

Location:

Comments:

Flower name: _____

Variety planted: _____

Seeds sown: _____

Germination period: _____

Seedlings planted out: _____

Location: _____

Comments: _____

_____

_____

Flower name: _____

Variety planted: _____

Seeds sown: _____

Germination period: _____

Seedlings planted out: _____

Location; _____

Comments: _____

_____

_____

Flower name: _____

Variety planted: _____

Seeds sown: _____

Germination period: _____

Seedlings planted out: _____

Location: _____

Comments: _____

_____

_____

Perennials

Flower name: _____

Variety planted: _____

Seeds sown: _____

Germination period: _____

Seedlings planted out: _____

Location: _____

Comments: _____

_____

_____

Flower name: _____

Variety planted: _____

Seeds sown: _____

Germination period: _____

Seedlings planted out: _____

Location: _____

Comments: _____

_____

_____

Flower name: _____

Variety planted: _____

Seeds sown: _____

Germination period: _____

Seedlings planted out: _____

Location: _____

Comments: _____

_____

_____

Flower name: _____

Variety planted: _____

Seeds sown: _____

Germination period: _____

Seedlings planted out: _____

Location: _____

Comments: _____

_____

_____

_____

Flower name: _____

Variety planted: _____

Seeds sown: _____

Germination period: _____

Seedlings planted out: _____

Location: _____

Comments: _____

_____

_____

_____

Flower name: _____

Variety planted: _____

Seeds sown: _____

Germination period: _____

Seedlings planted out: _____

Location: _____

Comments: _____

_____

_____

_____

Perennials

Flower name: _____

Variety planted: _____

Seeds sown: _____

Germination period: _____

Seedlings planted out: _____

Location: _____

Comments: _____

_____

_____

Flower name: _____

Variety planted: _____

Seeds sown: _____

Germination period: _____

Seedlings planted out: _____

Location: _____

Comments: _____

_____

_____

Flower name: _____

Variety planted: _____

Seeds sown: _____

Germination period: _____

Seedlings planted out: _____

Location: _____

Comments: _____

_____

_____

Flower name: _____

Variety planted: _____

Seeds sown: _____

Germination period: _____

Seedlings planted out: _____

Location: _____

Comments: _____

_____

_____

Flower name: _____

Variety planted: _____

Seeds sown: _____

Germination period: _____

Seedlings planted out: _____

Location; _____

Comments: _____

_____

_____

Flower name: _____

Variety planted: _____

Seeds sown: _____

Germination period: _____

Seedlings planted out: _____

Location: _____

Comments: _____

_____

_____

Perennials

Flower name: _____

Variety planted: _____

Seeds sown: _____

Germination period: _____

Seedlings planted out: _____

Location: _____

Comments: _____

_____

_____

_____

Flower name: _____

Variety planted: _____

Seeds sown: _____

Germination period: _____

Seedlings planted out: _____

Location: _____

Comments: _____

_____

_____

_____

Flower name: _____

Variety planted: _____

Seeds sown: _____

Germination period: _____

Seedlings planted out: _____

Location: _____

Comments: _____

_____

_____

_____

Flower name:

Variety planted:

Seeds sown:

Germination period:

Seedlings planted out:

Location:

Comments:

Flower name:

Variety planted:

Seeds sown:

Germination period:

Seedlings planted out:

Location;

Comments:

Flower name:

Variety planted:

Seeds sown:

Germination period:

Seedlings planted out:

Location:

Comments:

Perennials

Flower name:

Variety planted:

Seeds sown:

Germination period:

Seedlings planted out:

Location:

Comments:

Flower name:

Variety planted:

Seeds sown:

Germination period:

Seedlings planted out:

Location:

Comments:

Flower name:

Variety planted:

Seeds sown:

Germination period:

Seedlings planted out:

Location:

Comments:

Flower name: _____

Variety planted: _____

Seeds sown: _____

Germination period: _____

Seedlings planted out: _____

Location: _____

Comments: _____

_____

_____

Flower name: _____

Variety planted: _____

Seeds sown: _____

Germination period: _____

Seedlings planted out: _____

Location: _____

Comments: _____

_____

_____

Flower name: _____

Variety planted: _____

Seeds sown: _____

Germination period: _____

Seedlings planted out: _____

Location: _____

Comments: _____

_____

_____

Bulbs

Flower name: _____

Variety planted: _____

Bulbs planted: _____

Location: _____

Flowering period: _____

_____

Comments: _____

_____

_____

Flower name: _____

Variety planted: _____

Bulbs planted: _____

Location: _____

Flowering period: _____

_____

Comments: _____

_____

_____

Flower name: _____

Variety planted: _____

Bulbs planted: _____

Location: _____

Flowering period: _____

_____

Comments: _____

_____

_____

Flower name: _____

Variety planted: _____

Bulbs planted: _____

Location: _____

Flowering period: _____
_____

Comments: _____
_____
_____

Flower name: _____

Variety planted: _____

Bulbs planted: _____

Location: _____

Flowering period: _____
_____

Comments: _____
_____
_____

Flower name: _____

Variety planted: _____

Bulbs planted: _____

Location: _____

Flowering period: _____
_____

Comments: _____
_____
_____

Bulbs

Flower name:

Variety planted:

Bulbs planted:

Location:

Flowering period:

Comments:

Flower name:

Variety planted:

Bulbs planted:

Location:

Flowering period:

Comments:

Flower name:

Variety planted:

Bulbs planted:

Location:

Flowering period:

Comments:

Flower name: _____

Variety planted: _____

Bulbs planted: _____

Location: _____

Flowering period: _____

Comments: _____

_____

_____

Flower name: _____

Variety planted: _____

Bulbs planted: _____

Location: _____

Flowering period: _____

Comments: _____

_____

_____

Flower name: _____

Variety planted: _____

Bulbs planted: _____

Location: _____

Flowering period: _____

Comments: _____

_____

_____

Bulbs

Flower name:

Variety planted:

Bulbs planted:

Location:

Flowering period:

Comments:

Flower name:

Variety planted:

Bulbs planted:

Location:

Flowering period:

Comments:

Flower name:

Variety planted:

Bulbs planted:

Location:

Flowering period:

Comments:

Flower name: _____

Variety planted: _____

Bulbs planted: _____

Location: _____

Flowering period: _____
_____

Comments: _____
_____
_____
_____

Flower name: _____

Variety planted: _____

Bulbs planted: _____

Location: _____

Flowering period: _____
_____

Comments: _____
_____
_____
_____

Flower name: _____

Variety planted: _____

Bulbs planted: _____

Location: _____

Flowering period: _____
_____

Comments: _____
_____
_____
_____

Notes

JOHN A. SALZER SEED CO'S ESTABLISHMENT, LA CROSSE, WIS.

Trees & shrubs

Spring 1899

For some people, a garden simply isn't complete without trees to give height and shrubs to add interest all year round. When selecting a tree from a nursery or garden center, always check the maximum height it will grow to, and consider whether you want a tree to offer some shade, provide privacy, or add a burst of color with leaves or blossom.

It's just as important to select a tree's planting position in the garden carefully—bear in mind how far roots can travel underground and do not plant too close to the house or other buildings to avoid root damage. Ask advice, too, about how often your chosen tree will need pruning, and the best time of year to do this, and then note down in the following pages the dates that you carry this out. Make sure that you keep the blades of pruning shears and loppers sharp so that you can make clean cuts when pruning.

Shrubs can add structure to beds and borders and if you choose evergreen varieties, they will provide interesting focal points in the garden when other plants have died back in winter. Some varieties even flower during the colder months, making you feel that spring—and warmer weather—is on its way. As with trees, shrubs can benefit from regular trimming to keep them in shape and to encourage new growth.

Trees and shrubs

Tree/shrub name:
_____

Variety planted:
_____

Date planted:
_____

Pruning:
_____

Comments:
_____
_____

Tree/shrub name:
_____

Variety planted:
_____

Date planted:
_____

Pruning:
_____

Comments:
_____
_____

Tree/shrub name:
_____

Variety planted:
_____

Date planted:
_____

Pruning:
_____

Comments:
_____
_____

Tree/shrub name:
_____

Variety planted:
_____

Date planted:
_____

Pruning:
_____

Comments:
_____
_____

Tree/shrub name:

Variety planted:

Date planted:

Pruning:

Comments:

Tree/shrub name:

Variety planted:

Date planted:

Pruning:

Comments:

Tree/shrub name:

Variety planted:

Date planted:

Pruning:

Comments:

Tree/shrub name:

Variety planted:

Date planted:

Pruning:

Comments:

Trees and shrubs

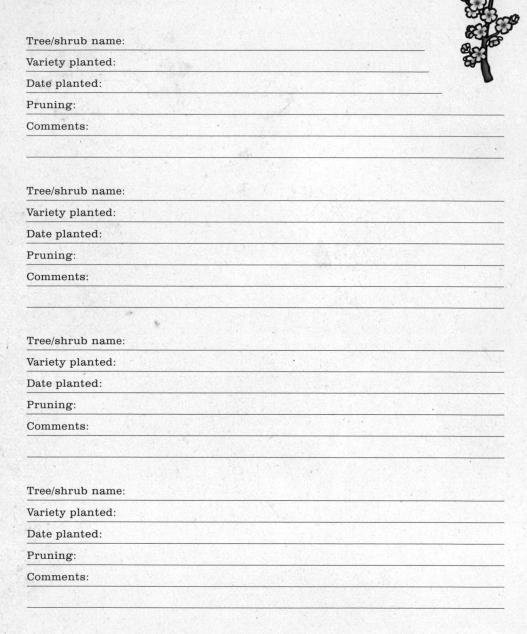

Tree/shrub name: _____

Variety planted: _____

Date planted: _____

Pruning: _____

Comments: _____

_____

Tree/shrub name: _____

Variety planted: _____

Date planted: _____

Pruning: _____

Comments: _____

_____

Tree/shrub name: _____

Variety planted: _____

Date planted: _____

Pruning: _____

Comments: _____

_____

Tree/shrub name: _____

Variety planted: _____

Date planted: _____

Pruning: _____

Comments: _____

_____

Tree/shrub name:

Variety planted:

Date planted:

Pruning:

Comments:

Tree/shrub name:

Variety planted:

Date planted:

Pruning:

Comments:

Tree/shrub name:

Variety planted:

Date planted:

Pruning:

Comments:

Tree/shrub name:

Variety planted:

Date planted:

Pruning:

Comments:

Trees and shrubs

Tree/shrub name: _____

Variety planted: _____

Date planted: _____

Pruning: _____

Comments: _____

_____

Tree/shrub name: _____

Variety planted: _____

Date planted: _____

Pruning: _____

Comments: _____

_____

Tree/shrub name: _____

Variety planted: _____

Date planted: _____

Pruning: _____

Comments: _____

_____

Tree/shrub name: _____

Variety planted: _____

Date planted: _____

Pruning: _____

Comments: _____

_____

Tree/shrub name: _____

Variety planted: _____

Date planted: _____

Pruning: _____

Comments: _____

_____

Tree/shrub name: _____

Variety planted: _____

Date planted: _____

Pruning: _____

Comments: _____

_____

Tree/shrub name: _____

Variety planted: _____

Date planted: _____

Pruning: _____

Comments: _____

_____

Tree/shrub name: _____

Variety planted: _____

Date planted: _____

Pruning: _____

Comments: _____

_____

Trees and shrubs

Tree/shrub name:

Variety planted:

Date planted:

Pruning:

Comments:

Tree/shrub name:

Variety planted:

Date planted:

Pruning:

Comments:

Tree/shrub name:

Variety planted:

Date planted:

Pruning:

Comments:

Tree/shrub name:

Variety planted:

Date planted:

Pruning:

Comments:

Tree/shrub name:

Variety planted:

Date planted:

Pruning:

Comments:

Tree/shrub name:

Variety planted:

Date planted:

Pruning:

Comments:

Tree/shrub name:

Variety planted:

Date planted:

Pruning:

Comments:

Tree/shrub name:

Variety planted:

Date planted:

Pruning:

Comments:

Notes

JOHN A. SALZER SEED CO'S ESTABLISHMENT, LA CROSSE, WIS.

 # *H*erbs

Spring 1899

As long as they have good soil, plenty of light, and a fair amount of sun and warmth, most herbs will thrive. If you are new to vegetable gardening, it is no bad thing to start by growing herbs. You will soon graduate to growing vegetables, and then you can put your herbs and vegetables together in the kitchen and create some delicious meals.

Among hardy perennial herbs that can survive at quite low temperatures are the alliums. This family includes chives, a useful everyday herb that is easy to grow and has pretty purple, edible flowers. Welsh onions are similar to chives but have rather bulbous hollow leaves; and garlic chives have straplike leaves and lovely white flowers.

Sweet marjoram, oregano, and thyme will tolerate dry conditions. Tarragon needs space, but is also worth growing—make sure you choose the French type, it has the best flavor. Rosemary and sage are larger evergreen shrubs with a woody framework and should be planted with a good depth of potting mix. Mint is also popular with gardeners— Korean and American mountain mints are good for making tea.

Annual herbs, which last for one season only, should be grown from seed. Indispensable varieties include basil, dill, and cilantro (coriander). Garden chervil is another annual herb, and is useful for cooking. Annuals will flower and set seed in a season.

Herbs

Herb name: _____

Variety planted: _____

Seeds sown: _____

Germination period: _____

Seedlings planted out: _____

Comments: _____

_____

_____

_____

_____

Herb name: _____

Variety planted: _____

Seeds sown: _____

Germination period: _____

Seedlings planted out: _____

Comments: _____

_____

_____

_____

_____

Herb name: _____

Variety planted: _____

Seeds sown: _____

Germination period: _____

Seedlings planted out: _____

Comments: _____

_____

_____

_____

Herb name: _____

Variety planted: _____

Seeds sown: _____

Germination period: _____

Seedlings planted out: _____

Comments: _____

_____

_____

_____

_____

Herb name: _____

Variety planted: _____

Seeds sown: _____

Germination period: _____

Seedlings planted out: _____

Comments: _____

_____

_____

_____

_____

Herb name: _____

Variety planted: _____

Seeds sown: _____

Germination period: _____

Seedlings planted out: _____

Comments: _____

_____

_____

_____

_____

Herbs

Herb name: _____

Variety planted: _____

Seeds sown: _____

Germination period: _____

Seedlings planted out: _____

Comments: _____

_____

_____

_____

_____

Herb name: _____

Variety planted: _____

Seeds sown: _____

Germination period: _____

Seedlings planted out: _____

Comments: _____

_____

_____

_____

_____

Herb name: _____

Variety planted: _____

Seeds sown: _____

Germination period: _____

Seedlings planted out: _____

Comments: _____

_____

_____

_____

Herb name: _____

Variety planted: _____

Seeds sown: _____

Germination period: _____

Seedlings planted out: _____

Comments: _____

_____

_____

_____

_____

Herb name: _____

Variety planted: _____

Seeds sown: _____

Germination period: _____

Seedlings planted out: _____

Comments: _____

_____

_____

_____

Herb name: _____

Variety planted: _____

Seeds sown: _____

Germination period: _____

Seedlings planted out: _____

Comments: _____

_____

_____

_____

Herbs

Herb name: _____

Variety planted: _____

Seeds sown: _____

Germination period: _____

Seedlings planted out: _____

Comments: _____

_____

_____

_____

Herb name: _____

Variety planted: _____

Seeds sown: _____

Germination period: _____

Seedlings planted out: _____

Comments: _____

_____

_____

_____

Herb name: _____

Variety planted: _____

Seeds sown: _____

Germination period: _____

Seedlings planted out: _____

Comments: _____

_____

_____

_____

Herb name:

Variety planted:

Seeds sown:

Germination period:

Seedlings planted out:

Comments:

Herb name:

Variety planted:

Seeds sown:

Germination period:

Seedlings planted out:

Comments:

Herb name:

Variety planted:

Seeds sown:

Germination period:

Seedlings planted out:

Comments:

Herbs

Herb name: _____

Variety planted: _____

Seeds sown: _____

Germination period: _____

Seedlings planted out: _____

Comments: _____

_____

_____

_____

Herb name: _____

Variety planted: _____

Seeds sown: _____

Germination period: _____

Seedlings planted out: _____

Comments: _____

_____

_____

_____

Herb name: _____

Variety planted: _____

Seeds sown: _____

Germination period: _____

Seedlings planted out: _____

Comments: _____

_____

_____

_____

Herb name:

Variety planted:

Seeds sown:

Germination period:

Seedlings planted out:

Comments:

Herb name:

Variety planted:

Seeds sown:

Germination period:

Seedlings planted out:

Comments:

Herb name:

Variety planted:

Seeds sown:

Germination period:

Seedlings planted out:

Comments:

Notes

John A. Salzer Seed Co's Establishment, La Crosse, Wis.

Fruits

Spring
1899

Even if you have only a small outdoor space, you can still grow some of your own fruit, either on a tree or in plant form. Many fruit-bearing plants grow happily in containers, and some orchard trees have been bred especially for this purpose. As a rule fruits suffer in cold conditions, so protect plants carefully from frost and winds and make sure they are in a position where they receive a decent amount of sunlight.

Grape vines thrive if grown in a warm, sunny place. They need enough soil to retain moisture, and should be pruned regularly to reduce leafy growth and promote a well-formed plant that will yield a fair harvest. A good nursery will advise on the best type of vine for your climate and conditions.

Strawberries are one of the easiest fruits to grow. Both cultivated strawberries and the wild or alpine type need to be kept moist and will tolerate some shade. Allow the berries to ripen fully to a dark red color, and pick them to eat straight from the plant.

Physalis (also called cape gooseberries) are easy to grow and generally not attacked by pests. Seeds germinate quickly, or you can buy young plants. Like tomatoes, to which they are closely related, physalis need warmth and sun to ripen.

All fruit will benefit from a weekly high-potash liquid feed when the fruit begins to mature. A tomato feed is ideal; organic varieties are readily available.

Tree fruit

Fruit name:

Variety planted:

Pruning:

Harvest:

Comments:

Fruit name:

Variety planted:

Pruning:

Harvest:

Comments:

Fruit name:

Variety planted:

Pruning:

Harvest:

Comments:

Fruit name: _____

Variety planted: _____

Pruning: _____

Harvest: _____

Comments: _____
_____
_____
_____

Fruit name: _____

Variety planted: _____

Pruning: _____

Harvest: _____

Comments: _____
_____
_____
_____

Fruit name: _____

Variety planted: _____

Pruning: _____

Harvest: _____

Comments: _____
_____
_____
_____

Tree fruit

Fruit name: _____

Variety planted: _____

Pruning: _____

Harvest: _____

_____

Comments: _____

_____

_____

_____

Fruit name: _____

Variety planted: _____

Pruning: _____

Harvest: _____

Comments: _____

_____

_____

_____

Fruit name: _____

Variety planted: _____

Pruning: _____

Harvest: _____

Comments: _____

_____

_____

_____

Fruit name: _____
Variety planted: _____
Pruning: _____
Harvest: _____

Comments: _____
_____
_____
_____

Fruit name: _____
Variety planted: _____
Pruning: _____
Harvest: _____

Comments: _____
_____
_____
_____

Fruit name: _____
Variety planted: _____
Pruning: _____
Harvest: _____

Comments: _____
_____
_____
_____

Tree fruit

Fruit name: _____

Variety planted: _____

Pruning: _____

Harvest: _____
_____

Comments: _____
_____
_____
_____
_____

Fruit name: _____

Variety planted: _____

Pruning: _____

Harvest: _____
_____

Comments: _____
_____
_____
_____

Fruit name: _____

Variety planted: _____

Pruning: _____

Harvest: _____
_____

Comments: _____
_____
_____
_____

Fruit name: _____

Variety planted: _____

Pruning: _____

Harvest: _____

_____

Comments: _____

_____

_____

_____

_____

Fruit name: _____

Variety planted: _____

Pruning: _____

Harvest: _____

_____

Comments: _____

_____

_____

_____

Fruit name: _____

Variety planted: _____

Pruning: _____

Harvest: _____

_____

Comments: _____

_____

_____

_____

Bush fruit

Fruit name:

Variety planted:

Pruning:

Harvest:

Comments:

Fruit name:

Variety planted:

Pruning:

Harvest:

Comments:

Fruit name:

Variety planted:

Pruning:

Harvest:

Comments:

Fruit name: _____

Variety planted: _____

Pruning: _____

Harvest: _____

_____

Comments: _____

_____

_____

_____

Fruit name: _____

Variety planted: _____

Pruning: _____

Harvest: _____

_____

Comments: _____

_____

_____

_____

Fruit name: _____

Variety planted: _____

Pruning: _____

Harvest: _____

_____

Comments: _____

_____

_____

_____

Bush fruit

Fruit name: _____

Variety planted: _____

Pruning: _____

Harvest: _____

_____

Comments: _____

_____

_____

_____

_____

Fruit name: _____

Variety planted: _____

Pruning: _____

Harvest: _____

_____

Comments: _____

_____

_____

_____

_____

Fruit name: _____

Variety planted: _____

Pruning: _____

Harvest: _____

_____

Comments: _____

_____

_____

_____

Fruit name: _____

Variety planted: _____

Pruning: _____

Harvest: _____

_____

Comments: _____

_____

_____

_____

Fruit name: _____

Variety planted: _____

Pruning: _____

Harvest: _____

_____

Comments: _____

_____

_____

_____

Fruit name: _____

Variety planted: _____

Pruning: _____

Harvest: _____

_____

Comments: _____

_____

_____

_____

Bush fruit

Fruit name: _____

Variety planted: _____

Pruning: _____

Harvest: _____

Comments: _____

_____

_____

_____

Fruit name: _____

Variety planted: _____

Pruning: _____

Harvest: _____

Comments: _____

_____

_____

_____

Fruit name: _____

Variety planted: _____

Pruning: _____

Harvest: _____

Comments: _____

_____

_____

_____

Fruit name:

Variety planted:

Pruning:

Harvest:

Comments:

Fruit name:

Variety planted:

Pruning:

Harvest:

Comments:

Fruit name:

Variety planted:

Pruning:

Harvest:

Comments:

Bush fruit

Fruit name: _____

Variety planted: _____

Pruning: _____

Harvest: _____
_____

Comments: _____
_____
_____
_____

Fruit name: _____

Variety planted: _____

Pruning: _____

Harvest: _____
_____

Comments: _____
_____
_____
_____

Fruit name: _____

Variety planted: _____

Pruning: _____

Harvest: _____
_____

Comments: _____
_____
_____
_____

Fruit name:

Variety planted:

Pruning:

Harvest:

Comments:

Fruit name:

Variety planted:

Pruning:

Harvest:

Comments:

Fruit name:

Variety planted:

Pruning:

Harvest:

Comments:

Notes

Vegetables

SPRING 1899

SALZER'S ODDLY ODD GOURDS.
sensational mixture of rare, strange, droll, curious,
ar, comical, fantastical, queer, comely, funny,
tle, long, thin, fat, round, oblong and oddly odd
gourds. Just the seed you will want to plant
e children and for your own fun and pleasure.
n free with each order. See page 1.
20 cents; 2 pkgs. 40 cents; 1 oz. 25 cents.

There are five main vegetable groups: root vegetables, salad leaves, brassicas, legumes, and onions. There are also smaller groups that include pumpkins and tomatoes, amongst others.

To successfully grow root vegetables, such as parsnips and radishes, the plants must have a steady source of nutrients in the soil, cool climate, and good drainage. Potatoes are a popular variety and achieve good yields in well-prepared soil, as will carrots and beets (beetroot).

Salad leaves are quick and relatively simple to cultivate. They are shallow-rooting and need regular watering in the evenings to stop the compost drying out; prolonged drought stunts the growth of salad plants, producing tough bitter leaves.

Brassicas include cabbages and broccoli. They tend to flourish in cool, moist conditions and will suffer if exposed to a lot of direct sunlight. Plant brassicas in the same patch in late fall/autumn—most varieties grow in the same environment.

Legumes include beans of all kinds and are easy to grow. They suffer from few pests or diseases and tolerate most weather conditions. Another advantage is that they are highly nutritious—for some varieties it's best to eat the young green pods, while for others you can leave them on the plant to ripen into beans to be dried for eating in winter.

Plants from the onion family are a good choice for novices as they generally do not need much watering or nutrients. One thing onions do like is sunlight—plant them in a bright spot and weed regularly to avoid blocking out the sun.

Root vegetables

Vegetable name:

Variety planted:

Seeds sown:

Germination period:

Seedlings planted out:

Harvest:

Comments:

Vegetable name:

Variety planted:

Seeds sown:

Germination period:

Seedlings planted out:

Harvest:

Comments:

Vegetable name:

Variety planted:

Seeds sown:

Germination period:

Seedlings planted out:

Harvest:

Comments:

Vegetable name:

Variety planted:

Seeds sown:

Germination period:

Seedlings planted out:

Harvest:

Comments:

Vegetable name:

Variety planted:

Seeds sown:

Germination period:

Seedlings planted out:

Harvest:

Comments:

Vegetable name:

Variety planted:

Seeds sown:

Germination period:

Seedlings planted out:

Harvest:

Comments:

Root vegetables

Vegetable name:

Variety planted:

Seeds sown:

Germination period:

Seedlings planted out:

Harvest:

Comments:

Vegetable name:

Variety planted:

Seeds sown:

Germination period:

Seedlings planted out:

Harvest:

Comments:

Vegetable name:

Variety planted:

Seeds sown:

Germination period:

Seedlings planted out:

Harvest:

Comments:

Vegetable name:

Variety planted:

Seeds sown:

Germination period:

Seedlings planted out:

Harvest:

Comments:

Vegetable name:

Variety planted:

Seeds sown:

Germination period:

Seedlings planted out:

Harvest:

Comments:

Vegetable name:

Variety planted:

Seeds sown:

Germination period:

Seedlings planted out:

Harvest:

Comments:

Root vegetables

Vegetable name: _____

Variety planted: _____

Seeds sown: _____

Germination period: _____

Seedlings planted out: _____

Harvest: _____

Comments: _____

_____

_____

Vegetable name: _____

Variety planted: _____

Seeds sown: _____

Germination period: _____

Seedlings planted out: _____

Harvest: _____

Comments: _____

_____

_____

Vegetable name: _____

Variety planted: _____

Seeds sown: _____

Germination period: _____

Seedlings planted out: _____

Harvest: _____

Comments: _____

_____

_____

Vegetable name: _____

Variety planted: _____

Seeds sown: _____

Germination period: _____

Seedlings planted out: _____

Harvest: _____

Comments: _____

_____

_____

_____

Vegetable name: _____

Variety planted: _____

Seeds sown: _____

Germination period: _____

Seedlings planted out: _____

Harvest: _____

Comments: _____

_____

_____

_____

Vegetable name: _____

Variety planted: _____

Seeds sown: _____

Germination period: _____

Seedlings planted out: _____

Harvest: _____

Comments: _____

_____

_____

_____

Legumes

Vegetable name: _____

Variety planted: _____

Seeds sown: _____

Germination period: _____

Seedlings planted out: _____

Harvest: _____

Comments: _____

_____

_____

Vegetable name: _____

Variety planted: _____

Seeds sown: _____

Germination period: _____

Seedlings planted out: _____

Harvest: _____

Comments: _____

_____

_____

Vegetable name: _____

Variety planted: _____

Seeds sown: _____

Germination period: _____

Seedlings planted out: _____

Harvest: _____

Comments: _____

_____

_____

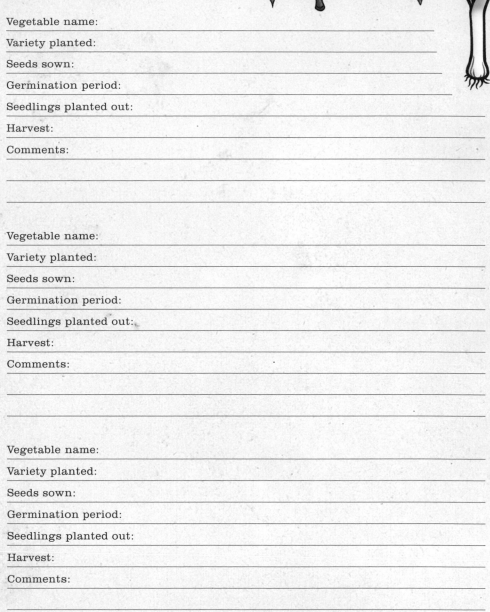

Vegetable name: _____

Variety planted: _____

Seeds sown: _____

Germination period: _____

Seedlings planted out: _____

Harvest: _____

Comments: _____

_____

_____

_____

Vegetable name: _____

Variety planted: _____

Seeds sown: _____

Germination period: _____

Seedlings planted out: _____

Harvest: _____

Comments: _____

_____

_____

_____

Vegetable name: _____

Variety planted: _____

Seeds sown: _____

Germination period: _____

Seedlings planted out: _____

Harvest: _____

Comments: _____

_____

_____

_____

Legumes

Vegetable name: _____

Variety planted: _____

Seeds sown: _____

Germination period: _____

Seedlings planted out: _____

Harvest: _____

Comments: _____

_____

_____

Vegetable name: _____

Variety planted: _____

Seeds sown: _____

Germination period: _____

Seedlings planted out: _____

Harvest: _____

Comments: _____

_____

_____

Vegetable name: _____

Variety planted: _____

Seeds sown: _____

Germination period: _____

Seedlings planted out: _____

Harvest: _____

Comments: _____

_____

_____

Vegetable name: _____

Variety planted: _____

Seeds sown: _____

Germination period: _____

Seedlings planted out: _____

Harvest: _____

Comments: _____

_____

_____

Vegetable name: _____

Variety planted: _____

Seeds sown: _____

Germination period: _____

Seedlings planted out: _____

Harvest: _____

Comments: _____

_____

_____

Vegetable name: _____

Variety planted: _____

Seeds sown: _____

Germination period: _____

Seedlings planted out: _____

Harvest: _____

Comments: _____

_____

_____

Legumes

Vegetable name: _____

Variety planted: _____

Seeds sown: _____

Germination period: _____

Seedlings planted out: _____

Harvest: _____

Comments: _____

_____

_____

Vegetable name: _____

Variety planted: _____

Seeds sown: _____

Germination period: _____

Seedlings planted out: _____

Harvest: _____

Comments: _____

_____

_____

Vegetable name: _____

Variety planted: _____

Seeds sown: _____

Germination period: _____

Seedlings planted out: _____

Harvest: _____

Comments: _____

_____

_____

Vegetable name: _____

Variety planted: _____

Seeds sown: _____

Germination period: _____

Seedlings planted out: _____

Harvest: _____

Comments: _____

_____

_____

Vegetable name: _____

Variety planted: _____

Seeds sown: _____

Germination period: _____

Seedlings planted out: _____

Harvest: _____

Comments: _____

_____

_____

Vegetable name: _____

Variety planted: _____

Seeds sown: _____

Germination period: _____

Seedlings planted out: _____

Harvest: _____

Comments: _____

_____

_____

Brassicas

Vegetable name: _____

Variety planted: _____

Seeds sown: _____

Germination period: _____

Seedlings planted out: _____

Harvest: _____

Comments: _____

_____

_____

Vegetable name: _____

Variety planted: _____

Seeds sown: _____

Germination period: _____

Seedlings planted out: _____

Harvest: _____

Comments: _____

_____

_____

Vegetable name: _____

Variety planted: _____

Seeds sown: _____

Germination period: _____

Seedlings planted out: _____

Harvest: _____

Comments: _____

_____

_____

Vegetable name: _____

Variety planted: _____

Seeds sown: _____

Germination period: _____

Seedlings planted out: _____

Harvest: _____

Comments: _____

_____

_____

Vegetable name: _____

Variety planted: _____

Seeds sown: _____

Germination period: _____

Seedlings planted out: _____

Harvest: _____

Comments: _____

_____

_____

Vegetable name: _____

Variety planted: _____

Seeds sown: _____

Germination period: _____

Seedlings planted out: _____

Harvest: _____

Comments: _____

_____

_____

Brassicas

Vegetable name:

Variety planted:

Seeds sown:

Germination period:

Seedlings planted out:

Harvest:

Comments:

Vegetable name:

Variety planted:

Seeds sown:

Germination period:

Seedlings planted out:

Harvest:

Comments:

Vegetable name:

Variety planted:

Seeds sown:

Germination period:

Seedlings planted out:

Harvest:

Comments:

Vegetable name: _____

Variety planted: _____

Seeds sown: _____

Germination period: _____

Seedlings planted out: _____

Harvest: _____

Comments: _____

_____

_____

_____

Vegetable name: _____

Variety planted: _____

Seeds sown: _____

Germination period: _____

Seedlings planted out: _____

Harvest: _____

Comments: _____

_____

_____

_____

Vegetable name: _____

Variety planted: _____

Seeds sown: _____

Germination period: _____

Seedlings planted out: _____

Harvest: _____

Comments: _____

_____

_____

_____

Brassicas

Vegetable name:
_____

Variety planted:
_____

Seeds sown:
_____

Germination period:
_____

Seedlings planted out:
_____

Harvest:
_____

Comments:
_____
_____
_____

Vegetable name:
_____

Variety planted:
_____

Seeds sown:
_____

Germination period:
_____

Seedlings planted out:
_____

Harvest:
_____

Comments:
_____
_____
_____

Vegetable name:
_____

Variety planted:
_____

Seeds sown:
_____

Germination period:
_____

Seedlings planted out:
_____

Harvest:
_____

Comments:
_____
_____
_____

Vegetable name: _____

Variety planted: _____

Seeds sown: _____

Germination period: _____

Seedlings planted out: _____

Harvest: _____

Comments: _____

_____

_____

Vegetable name: _____

Variety planted: _____

Seeds sown: _____

Germination period: _____

Seedlings planted out: _____

Harvest: _____

Comments: _____

_____

_____

Vegetable name: _____

Variety planted: _____

Seeds sown: _____

Germination period: _____

Seedlings planted out: _____

Harvest: _____

Comments: _____

_____

_____

Salad leaves

Vegetable name: _____

Variety planted: _____

Seeds sown: _____

Germination period: _____

Seedlings planted out: _____

Harvest: _____

Comments: _____

_____

_____

Vegetable name: _____

Variety planted: _____

Seeds sown: _____

Germination period: _____

Seedlings planted out: _____

Harvest: _____

Comments: _____

_____

_____

Vegetable name: _____

Variety planted: _____

Seeds sown: _____

Germination period: _____

Seedlings planted out: _____

Harvest: _____

Comments: _____

_____

_____

Vegetable name:

Variety planted:

Seeds sown:

Germination period:

Seedlings planted out:

Harvest:

Comments:

Vegetable name:

Variety planted:

Seeds sown:

Germination period:

Seedlings planted out:

Harvest:

Comments:

Vegetable name:

Variety planted:

Seeds sown:

Germination period:

Seedlings planted out:

Harvest:

Comments:

Salad leaves

Vegetable name: _____

Variety planted: _____

Seeds sown: _____

Germination period: _____

Seedlings planted out: _____

Harvest: _____

Comments: _____

_____

_____

Vegetable name: _____

Variety planted: _____

Seeds sown: _____

Germination period: _____

Seedlings planted out: _____

Harvest: _____

Comments: _____

_____

_____

Vegetable name: _____

Variety planted: _____

Seeds sown: _____

Germination period: _____

Seedlings planted out: _____

Harvest: _____

Comments: _____

_____

_____

Vegetable name: _____

Variety planted: _____

Seeds sown: _____

Germination period: _____

Seedlings planted out: _____

Harvest: _____

Comments: _____

_____

_____

Vegetable name: _____

Variety planted: _____

Seeds sown: _____

Germination period: _____

Seedlings planted out: _____

Harvest: _____

Comments: _____

_____

_____

Vegetable name: _____

Variety planted: _____

Seeds sown: _____

Germination period: _____

Seedlings planted out: _____

Harvest: _____

Comments: _____

_____

_____

Salad leaves

Vegetable name:

Variety planted:

Seeds sown:

Germination period:

Seedlings planted out:

Harvest:

Comments:

Vegetable name:

Variety planted:

Seeds sown:

Germination period:

Seedlings planted out:

Harvest:

Comments:

Vegetable name:

Variety planted:

Seeds sown:

Germination period:

Seedlings planted out:

Harvest:

Comments:

Vegetable name: _____

Variety planted: _____

Seeds sown: _____

Germination period: _____

Seedlings planted out: _____

Harvest: _____

Comments: _____

_____

_____

Vegetable name: _____

Variety planted: _____

Seeds sown: _____

Germination period: _____

Seedlings planted out: _____

Harvest: _____

Comments: _____

_____

_____

Vegetable name: _____

Variety planted: _____

Seeds sown: _____

Germination period: _____

Seedlings planted out: _____

Harvest: _____

Comments: _____

_____

_____

Onions

Vegetable name: _____

Variety planted: _____

Seeds sown: _____

Germination period: _____

Seedlings planted out: _____

Harvest: _____

Comments: _____

_____

_____

Vegetable name: _____

Variety planted: _____

Seeds sown: _____

Germination period: _____

Seedlings planted out: _____

Harvest: _____

Comments: _____

_____

_____

Vegetable name: _____

Variety planted: _____

Seeds sown: _____

Germination period: _____

Seedlings planted out: _____

Harvest: _____

Comments: _____

_____

_____

Vegetable name:

Variety planted:

Seeds sown:

Germination period:

Seedlings planted out:

Harvest:

Comments:

Vegetable name:

Variety planted:

Seeds sown:

Germination period:

Seedlings planted out:

Harvest:

Comments:

Vegetable name:

Variety planted:

Seeds sown:

Germination period:

Seedlings planted out:

Harvest:

Comments:

Onions

Vegetable name: _____

Variety planted: _____

Seeds sown: _____

Germination period: _____

Seedlings planted out: _____

Harvest: _____

Comments: _____

_____

_____

Vegetable name: _____

Variety planted: _____

Seeds sown: _____

Germination period: _____

Seedlings planted out: _____

Harvest: _____

Comments: _____

_____

_____

Vegetable name: _____

Variety planted: _____

Seeds sown: _____

Germination period: _____

Seedlings planted out: _____

Harvest: _____

Comments: _____

_____

_____

Vegetable name:

Variety planted:

Seeds sown:

Germination period:

Seedlings planted out:

Harvest:

Comments:

Vegetable name:

Variety planted:

Seeds sown:

Germination period:

Seedlings planted out:

Harvest:

Comments:

Vegetable name:

Variety planted:

Seeds sown:

Germination period:

Seedlings planted out:

Harvest:

Comments:

Other Vegetables

Vegetable name:

Variety planted:

Seeds sown:

Germination period:

Seedlings planted out:

Harvest:

Comments:

_____

_____

Vegetable name:

Variety planted:

Seeds sown:

Germination period:

Seedlings planted out:

Harvest:

Comments:

_____

_____

Vegetable name:

Variety planted:

Seeds sown:

Germination period:

Seedlings planted out:

Harvest:

Comments:

_____

_____

Vegetable name: _____

Variety planted: _____

Seeds sown: _____

Germination period: _____

Seedlings planted out: _____

Harvest: _____

Comments: _____

_____

_____

Vegetable name: _____

Variety planted: _____

Seeds sown: _____

Germination period: _____

Seedlings planted out: _____

Harvest: _____

Comments: _____

_____

_____

Vegetable name: _____

Variety planted: _____

Seeds sown: _____

Germination period: _____

Seedlings planted out: _____

Harvest: _____

Comments: _____

_____

_____

Other Vegetables

Vegetable name: _____

Variety planted: _____

Seeds sown: _____

Germination period: _____

Seedlings planted out: _____

Harvest: _____

Comments: _____

_____

_____

Vegetable name: _____

Variety planted: _____

Seeds sown: _____

Germination period: _____

Seedlings planted out: _____

Harvest: _____

Comments: _____

_____

_____

Vegetable name: _____

Variety planted: _____

Seeds sown: _____

Germination period: _____

Seedlings planted out: _____

Harvest: _____

Comments: _____

_____

_____

Vegetable name: _____

Variety planted: _____

Seeds sown: _____

Germination period: _____

Seedlings planted out: _____

Harvest: _____

Comments: _____

_____

_____

Vegetable name: _____

Variety planted: _____

Seeds sown: _____

Germination period: _____

Seedlings planted out: _____

Harvest: _____

Comments: _____

_____

_____

Vegetable name: _____

Variety planted: _____

Seeds sown: _____

Germination period: _____

Seedlings planted out: _____

Harvest: _____

Comments: _____

_____

_____

Other Vegetables

Vegetable name:

Variety planted:

Seeds sown:

Germination period:

Seedlings planted out:

Harvest:

Comments:

Vegetable name:

Variety planted:

Seeds sown:

Germination period:

Seedlings planted out:

Harvest:

Comments:

Vegetable name:

Variety planted:

Seeds sown:

Germination period:

Seedlings planted out:

Harvest:

Comments:

Vegetable name: _____

Variety planted: _____

Seeds sown: _____

Germination period: _____

Seedlings planted out: _____

Harvest: _____

Comments: _____

_____

_____

Vegetable name: _____

Variety planted: _____

Seeds sown: _____

Germination period: _____

Seedlings planted out: _____

Harvest: _____

Comments: _____

_____

_____

Vegetable name: _____

Variety planted: _____

Seeds sown: _____

Germination period: _____

Seedlings planted out: _____

Harvest: _____

Comments: _____

_____

_____

Other Vegetables

Vegetable name: _____

Variety planted: _____

Seeds sown: _____

Germination period: _____

Seedlings planted out: _____

Harvest: _____

Comments: _____

_____

_____

Vegetable name: _____

Variety planted: _____

Seeds sown: _____

Germination period: _____

Seedlings planted out: _____

Harvest: _____

Comments: _____

_____

_____

Vegetable name: _____

Variety planted: _____

Seeds sown: _____

Germination period: _____

Seedlings planted out: _____

Harvest: _____

Comments: _____

_____

_____

Vegetable name: _____

Variety planted: _____

Seeds sown: _____

Germination period: _____

Seedlings planted out: _____

Harvest: _____

Comments: _____

_____

_____

Vegetable name: _____

Variety planted: _____

Seeds sown: _____

Germination period: _____

Seedlings planted out: _____

Harvest: _____

Comments: _____

_____

_____

Vegetable name: _____

Variety planted: _____

Seeds sown: _____

Germination period: _____

Seedlings planted out: _____

Harvest: _____

Comments: _____

_____

_____

Notes

Chapter 3

Weekly diary

Week 1   Date:

_____
_____
_____
_____
_____
_____
_____
_____
_____
_____
_____
_____
_____
_____
_____
_____
_____
_____
_____
_____
_____
_____

Week 2   Date:

_____

_____

_____

_____

_____

_____

_____

_____

_____

_____

_____

_____

_____

_____

_____

_____

_____

_____

_____

_____

_____

_____

Week 3   Date:

_____

_____

_____

_____

_____

_____

_____

_____

_____

_____

_____

_____

_____

_____

_____

_____

_____

_____

_____

_____

_____

_____

_____

Week 4   Date:

_____

_____

_____

_____

_____

_____

_____

_____

_____

_____

_____

_____

_____

_____

_____

_____

_____

_____

Week 5   Date:

Week 6   Date:

_____

_____

_____

_____

_____

_____

_____

_____

_____

_____

_____

_____

_____

_____

_____

_____

_____

_____

_____

_____

_____

_____

Week 7   Date:

_____

_____

_____

_____

_____

_____

_____

_____

_____

_____

_____

_____

_____

_____

_____

_____

_____

_____

_____

_____

Week 8   Date:

_____
_____
_____
_____
_____
_____
_____
_____
_____
_____
_____
_____
_____
_____
_____
_____
_____
_____
_____
_____

Week 9   Date:

_____

_____

_____

_____

_____

_____

_____

_____

_____

_____

_____

_____

_____

_____

_____

_____

_____

_____

_____

_____

Week 10   Date:

_____

_____

_____

_____

_____

_____

_____

_____

_____

_____

_____

_____

_____

_____

_____

_____

_____

_____

_____

_____

_____

_____

Week 11   Date:

Week 12   Date:

_____

_____

_____

_____

_____

_____

_____

_____

_____

_____

_____

_____

_____

_____

_____

_____

_____

_____

_____

_____

Week 13   Date:

Week 14   Date:

_____
_____
_____
_____
_____
_____
_____
_____
_____
_____
_____
_____
_____
_____
_____
_____
_____
_____
_____
_____
_____
_____
_____

Week 15   Date:

_____

_____

_____

_____

_____

_____

_____

_____

_____

_____

_____

_____

_____

_____

_____

_____

_____

_____

_____

_____

Week 16   Date:

Week 17   Date:

Week 18   Date:

Week 19   Date:

___

Week 20   Date:

_____

_____

_____

_____

_____

_____

_____

_____

_____

_____

_____

_____

_____

_____

_____

_____

_____

_____

_____

Week 21   Date:

Week 22   Date:

_____

_____

_____

_____

_____

_____

_____

_____

_____

_____

_____

_____

_____

_____

_____

_____

_____

_____

_____

_____

_____

Week 23   Date:

Week 24   Date:

Week 25   Date:

_____
_____
_____
_____
_____
_____
_____
_____
_____
_____
_____
_____
_____
_____
_____
_____
_____
_____
_____
_____
_____
_____

Week 26   Date:

_____

_____

_____

_____

_____

_____

_____

_____

_____

_____

_____

_____

_____

_____

_____

_____

_____

_____

_____

_____

_____

_____

Week 27   Date:

Week 28   Date:

Week 29   Date:

Week 30   Date:

Week 31   Date:

Week 32   Date:

Week 33   Date:

_____

_____

_____

_____

_____

_____

_____

_____

_____

_____

_____

_____

_____

_____

_____

_____

_____

_____

_____

_____

_____

_____

Week 34 　　Date:

Week 35   Date:

_____

_____

_____

_____

_____

_____

_____

_____

_____

_____

_____

_____

_____

_____

_____

_____

_____

_____

_____

_____

Week 36   Date:

_____

_____

_____

_____

_____

_____

_____

_____

_____

_____

_____

_____

_____

_____

_____

_____

_____

Week 37   Date:

_____

_____

_____

_____

_____

_____

_____

_____

_____

_____

_____

_____

_____

_____

_____

_____

_____

_____

_____

_____

_____

_____

Week 38   Date:

Week 39   Date:

Week 40   Date:

Week 41   Date:

_____

_____

_____

_____

_____

_____

_____

_____

_____

_____

_____

_____

_____

_____

_____

_____

_____

_____

_____

_____

_____

_____

_____

_____

Week 42   Date:

_____

_____

_____

_____

_____

_____

_____

_____

_____

_____

_____

_____

_____

_____

_____

_____

_____

_____

_____

_____

_____

Week 43   Date:

Week 44   Date:

_____
_____
_____
_____
_____
_____
_____
_____
_____
_____
_____
_____
_____
_____
_____
_____
_____
_____
_____
_____
_____

Week 46   Date:

Week 47   Date:

Week 48   Date:

Week 49   Date:

_____
_____
_____
_____
_____
_____
_____
_____
_____
_____
_____
_____
_____
_____
_____
_____
_____
_____
_____
_____

Week 50   Date:

Week 51   Date:

Week 52   Date:

Chapter 4

Keeping organized

Garden visits

When visiting gardens, note down any interesting plant varieties you would like to research in the future.

Garden name: _____

Date visited: _____

Favorite plants: _____

_____

_____

Notes: _____

_____

_____

_____

_____

Garden name: _____

Date visited: _____

Favorite plants: _____

_____

_____

Notes: _____

_____

_____

_____

_____

Garden name: _____

Date visited: _____

Favorite plants: _____

_____

_____

Notes: _____

_____

_____

_____

Garden name:

Date visited:

Favorite plants:

Notes:

Garden name:

Date visited:

Favorite plants:

Notes:

Garden name:

Date visited:

Favorite plants:

Notes:

Garden visits

Garden name: _____

Date visited: _____

Favorite plants: _____

_____

_____

Notes: _____

_____

_____

_____

_____

Garden name: _____

Date visited: _____

Favorite plants: _____

_____

_____

Notes: _____

_____

_____

_____

_____

Garden name: _____

Date visited: _____

Favorite plants: _____

_____

_____

Notes: _____

_____

_____

_____

_____

Garden name: _____

Date visited: _____

Favorite plants: _____

_____

_____

Notes: _____

_____

_____

_____

Garden name: _____

Date visited: _____

Favorite plants: _____

_____

_____

Notes: _____

_____

_____

_____

Garden name: _____

Date visited: _____

Favorite plants: _____

_____

_____

Notes: _____

_____

_____

_____

Address book

Name:

Tel:

Address:

Email/website:

Name:

Tel:

Address:

Email/website:

Name:

Tel:

Address:

Email/website:

Name:

Tel:

Address:

Email/website:

Name:

Tel:

Address:

Email/website:

Name:

Tel:

Address:

Email/website:

Name:

Tel:

Address:

Email/website:

Name:

Tel:

Address:

Email/website:

Name:

Tel:

Address:

Email/website:

Name:

Tel:

Address:

Email/website:

Address book

Name:

Tel:

Address:

Email/website:

Name:

Tel:

Address:

Email/website:

Name:

Tel:

Address:

Email/website:

Name:

Tel:

Address:

Email/website:

Name:

Tel:

Address:

Email/website:

Name:

Tel:

Address:

Email/website:

Name:

Tel:

Address:

Email/website:

Name:

Tel:

Address:

Email/website:

Name:

Tel:

Address:

Email/website:

Name:

Tel:

Address:

Email/website:

Useful gardening websites

www.
Notes:

www.
Notes:

www.
Notes:

www.
Notes:

www.
Notes:

www.
Notes:

www.

Notes:

www.

Notes:

www.

Notes:

www.

Notes:

www.

Notes:

www.

Notes:

Picture credits